Chocolate

More Than 50 Decadent Recipes

DOMINIQUE AND CINDY DUBY

DEFINITIVE KITCHEN CLASSICS

whitecap

Edited by Paula Ayer
Proofread by Sarah Maitland
Interior design by Janine Vangool
Typeset by Mauve Pagé
Food styling and photography ©2009
  by Dominique and Cindy Duby
Printed in China

Library and Archives Canada Cataloguing in Publication

Duby, Dominique, 1961–

　　Chocolate / Dominique and Cindy Duby.

ISBN 978-1-77050-001-3

　　1. Cookery (Chocolate). 2. Chocolate desserts. 3. Chocolate.

I. Duby, Cindy, 1960– II. Title.

TX767.C5D8155 2009　　　641.6'374
　C2009-902682-1

The publisher acknowledges the financial support of the Government of Canada through the Book Publishing Industry Development Program (BPIDP) and the Province of British Columbia through the Book Publishing Tax Credit.

09 10 11 12 13　　5 4 3 2 1

TABLE OF CONTENTS

CHOCOLATE BEGAN AS A BITTER TREAT OF RAW, POUNDED COCOA BEANS THAT THE AZTECS CHEWED WITH A LITTLE WATER. HOW FAR IT HAS COME!

To make chocolate today, cocoa beans are removed from their pods, then fermented, dried, roasted, cracked, and winnowed to separate the nibs from the husks. Next, grinding liquefies the nibs into a thick, dark paste called chocolate liquor. The chocolate liquor is mixed with sugar (and milk products for milk chocolate), then the mixture is refined before going through a process called *conching*. During this process, huge machines with rotating blades slowly blend the heated chocolate liquor to remove residual moisture and acids, and as the machines work their magic, they turn a largely bitter liquid into pure, smooth chocolate. The flavor and texture of the chocolate are determined by the type and origin of the cocoa beans, the fermentation process, and the ratio of roasting time to temperature, as well as the length of conching time.

Quite a few large chocolate manufacturers, including Lindt & Sprüngli, from Switzerland, and Valrhona, from France, produce widely available, high-quality chocolate bars. The bars are labeled by the percentage of cocoa they contain and/or the origin of the cocoa beans. The world of chocolate, like the wine industry a few years ago, is burgeoning with an increasing number of small artisanal chocolate makers who craft their own chocolate, from cocoa bean to bar. These artisans are not to be confused with the many chocolatiers who buy bulk chocolate from large chocolate manufacturers to make bars, which they then sell as their "own" chocolate. You are much better off buying Lindt or Valrhona bars, as they will most likely be the same product, but for a lot less money.

At our company, DC DUBY Wild Sweets®, which has emerged as one of North America's finest artisanal chocolatiers, we continually strive to push the envelope of creativity while making one of the world's great chocolates—whether for our Virtual Chocolate Boutique or for our exclusive retail line of chocolates for gourmet grocers and fine food boutiques. Our great interest in understanding the art and science of the chocolate-making process led us to become, in 2009, one of the few companies in the world to produce original chocolate bars from the world's very best cocoa beans in our own laboratory, on a microbatch basis—in true small-scale artisan fashion (see the Resources section).

As with wine pairing, which is also covered in this book, we encourage you to experiment with chocolates from different manufacturers and artisanal chocolate makers, and with various cocoa percentages and bean origins. Not only will this allow you to determine what you like best, but you'll also experience how much using different base chocolates can affect the end result of a dessert or confection. Keep in mind that even if you have the best recipe for the most delicious chocolate dessert, if it is made with an inferior chocolate, the dessert will never deliver its full sensory potential.

Chocolate 101

SELECTING

There are many varieties and brands of chocolate available to choose from, so it may be difficult to know what kind to buy. The most important factor in obtaining a successful result with chocolate is its quality. The type of beans and percentage of cocoa liquor, as well as the quality and quantity of the added ingredients (such as sugar, milk powder, or flavoring) largely determines the flavor of the chocolate. For example, too much fat results in a less intense and cloying chocolate, whereas too much sugar inhibits the chocolate flavor. To get the best results, you should understand the factors that define quality and differentiate one type of chocolate from another. Things to consider when buying chocolate:

- **LOOK** for signs of freshness. Check the expiry date and buy only what you can consume within a couple of weeks. Look for signs of fat bloom—pale gray streaks and blotches on the surface of the chocolate. This indicates that the chocolate has been exposed to overly warm temperatures (including sunlight near a window, or a hot lamp) and the cocoa butter is rising to the surface. Also, look for signs of sugar bloom—gray sugar crystals forming on the surface of the chocolate, which indicate that it has been exposed to dampness or condensation. The chocolate should be shiny and without blemishes, and it should break cleanly without crumbling.

- **SMELL** the chocolate. A well-rounded aroma is what you want. Chocolate easily picks up odors from products it is stored near (from laundry soap to onions), so keep unused portions of chocolate well wrapped, in an airtight container, and away from strong odors.

- **LISTEN** for a loud, crisp break when you bite into a piece of chocolate.

- **FEEL** the chocolate in your mouth. It should melt easily without clinging to your palate. It should be smooth and creamy on the tongue and release its distinctive notes and flavors.

There are several types of chocolate available, differentiated by their production formula (percentage of chocolate liquor, sugar content, and whether they contain dairy products). Here is a list of factors to consider when selecting what type of chocolate to use:

- **UNSWEETENED OR BAKING CHOCOLATE** typically contains no sugar and is used for baking. We rarely use this type of chocolate in our recipes; instead, we prefer to use cocoa powder if we want to increase the chocolate flavor in sorbets, cake mixes, or other desserts.

- **DARK CHOCOLATE** is usually labeled either as bittersweet or semisweet chocolate, depending on the amount of sugar added by the manufacturer. It contains anywhere from 35 percent to 99 percent combined cocoa solids (chocolate liquor and cocoa butter). The higher the percentage, the more bitter the chocolate. Typically, this type of chocolate is used for fillings, mousses, custards, and soufflés or other cakes with a soft texture. You should look for a chocolate that has a good balance of strong cocoa notes with just enough sugar; it should be more bitter than sweet. Select a 70-percent-cocoa dark chocolate with a deep, intense, bitter cocoa flavor, light acidic notes, and a long-lasting intensity in the mouth.

- **MILK CHOCOLATE** is the type of chocolate most popular in North America. It should contain at least 12 percent milk solids. This type of chocolate is normally used for fillings, mousses, custards, and parfaits. You should look for a chocolate that is well balanced—not too sweet, but with noticeable cocoa and dairy notes—and that melts easily. Select a milk chocolate with caramel and full-cream flavors that has a creamy and smooth feel in the mouth.

- **WHITE CHOCOLATE** does not contain any cocoa liquor, only cocoa butter. Therefore it is not technically a chocolate product. As white chocolate contains a lot of milk solids, select a chocolate that is cream or ivory in color, which indicates that it contains a higher percentage of cocoa butter. This type of chocolate is used for fillings, mousses, custards, and soft-textured cakes, as well as to add sweetness to recipes. You should look for a chocolate that has characteristics similar to good-quality milk chocolate, and that is not too sweet or thick. It should have distinct fresh milk and butter flavors and a smooth and creamy texture.

- **COCOA NIBS** are pieces of whole cocoa beans that have been roasted, cracked, and winnowed (bean husk removed). These nibs are the purest form of chocolate as they are unprocessed and contain no added ingredients. Cocoa nibs add great texture to a dish or confection, and are a great alternative to roasted nuts.

TEMPERING

Chocolate used for coating confections or to make decorations must be tempered in order to have the characteristics described above. Tempering is the process of stabilizing a chocolate mass through melting and cooling at specific temperatures until the right type of crystals are formed. First, the chocolate is heated so that all existing cocoa butter crystals are melted.

Next, it is cooled so that different cocoa butter crystals can form and grow. (The chocolate needs to be agitated/stirred for at least 5 minutes; it will become thicker and more viscous as the crystals form.) Finally, the chocolate is warmed to stabilize the crystals, making it fluid and ready to use. The optimum temperatures for the three types of chocolate at each stage of the tempering process are as follows:

	HEATING (STAGE 1)	COOLING (STAGE 2)	WARMING (STAGE 3)
Dark	113°F (45°C)	85°F (29°C)	90°F (32°C)
Milk	113°F (45°C)	83°F (28°C)	86°F (30°C)
White	113°F (45°C)	81°F (27°C)	85°F (29°C)

Tempering machines are highly recommended for melting and warming up chocolate, but if you do not have one, use a microwave, following the method below. (As a last resort, you can use a *bain marie* (water bath/double boiler), although you must be very, very careful about exposing the chocolate to any moisture including steam!). An accurate instant-read thermometer is crucial. Note that tempering is a very tricky process, and that even home tempering machines will not always succeed (see next page).

Expert chocolatiers will use very high-tech equipment to ensure the entire amount of chocolate is brought to very specific temperatures, but there is a slightly altered method that the home chef can follow, using the microwave (also called the *injection* method). Heat two-thirds of the (chopped) chocolate in short intervals at medium power, stirring between each interval, until it reaches 113°F (45°C). Finely chop the remaining third and add it to the melted mixture. Stir until the mixture is smooth, homogenous, and at the optimum temperature for stage 3. (You do not have to worry about stage 2.)

Another variation is the *table method*. Heat the chocolate to 113°F (45°C) and pour half of it onto a clean, dry, cool marble or stainless steel slab. Using a spatula, quickly move the mixture back and forth on the cool surface until it thickens and becomes like corn syrup in consistency. Quickly scrape it back into the remaining half of the chocolate and stir for at least 5 minutes until the entire mixture is at stage 3. If the mixture is too warm, repeat with a smaller amount. If the mixture is too cold, warm up to stage 3. (Use a hair dryer to blow hot air on the chocolate while stirring.)

Successfully tempered and set chocolate will shine, snap, and contract. Water is chocolate's number-one enemy, so ensure that all utensils and surfaces are completely free of moisture when tempering.

Chocolate can also be tempered mechanically using a tempering machine. Although commercial units can be very big and expensive, there are reasonably priced tabletop chocolate temperers to use at home. If you are planning to start making candies on a regular basis, then buying such a machine may be worth the investment. Several companies (such as ACMC and Chocovision) offer models that can temper from 1½ to 6 pounds (500 g to 2.7 kg) of chocolate, and that range in price from $350 to over $1,000. Models come with LED or LCD screens, are heated using forced hot air that is fully controlled by a thermostat, and can automatically temper melted chocolate in about 30 minutes.

Although tempering using a machine is a lot more convenient, it is by no means foolproof. Even with a good-quality tempering machine, there is no guarantee that your chocolate will be perfectly tempered. Conditions such as room temperature and humidity, for example, can affect the tempering process, whether it is done mechanically or manually.

Tempered chocolate can be used to make molded confections, or to dip or coat fillings. The finished products should be stored in a cool, dry place with a constant temperature no higher than 68°F (20°C). Storing at 54 to 57°F (12 to 14°C) is best.

EMULSIONS

The filling in molded or coated chocolate confections or cakes is often referred to as *ganache*, but it is in fact an emulsion. Emulsifying is the process of mixing two ingredients that typically do not combine (i.e., a liquid and a fat) into a stable homogenous mixture. The ingredients are forced together and held in suspension through the manual or mechanical action of beating, whisking, or mixing. In chocolate emulsions, cocoa butter is the fat and cream is the liquid. Emulsions are very prone to separation, so it is important to use a correct formula to combine these two elements. If a formula does not have the proper ratio of cocoa butter to cream, or has too much sugar (whether added or from the chocolate itself), the emulsion will not yield a ganache that is smooth, shiny, elastic, and firm enough to be cut.

Incorrect temperature is the next major cause of separation. Once the hot cream is poured over the chopped chocolate, and at all times during the emulsification process, the mixture must remain at a temperature higher than 95°F (35°C)—the point of fusion of cocoa butter—and preferably between 95 and 105°F (35 and 40°C). For best results, we recommend making the emulsion in a tall, narrow container using an immersion blender. If the formula calls for butter and/or alcohol, they should be added after the emulsion is complete, and in that order.

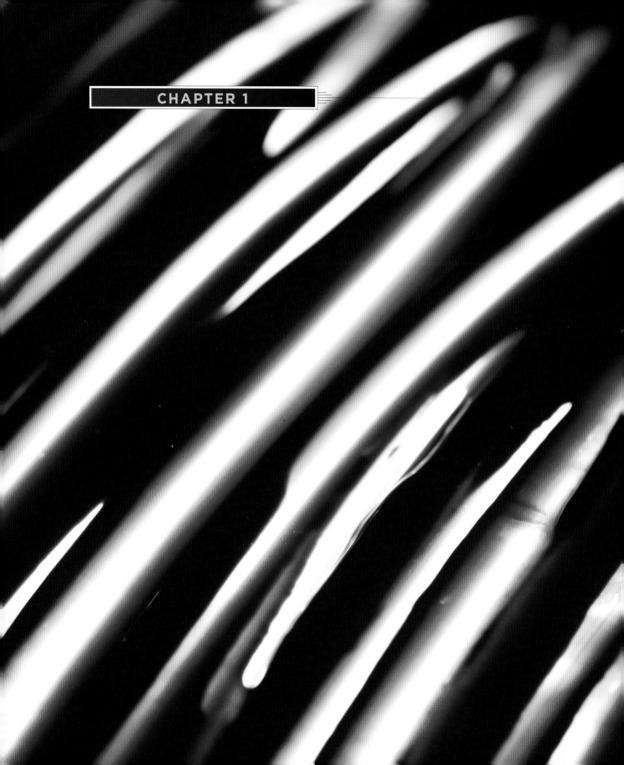

CHAPTER 1

Light & Liquid

Chocolate Fondue with Strawberries & Cake

FONDUE

1 cup (250 mL) whipping cream

7.2 oz (200 g) 70% dark chocolate,
finely chopped

kirsch or orange liqueur to taste (optional)

GARNISH

1 Tbsp + 2 tsp (25 mL) whipping cream

¼ cup (60 g) mascarpone cheese

TO SERVE

wooden skewers

½ of a pound cake, cut into bite-sized pieces

12–18 strawberries, hulled and quartered

2–3 Tbsp (25–30 g) sliced almonds, toasted

sprigs mint

For the fondue, bring whipping cream to a boil in a heavy saucepan. Place chocolate in a bowl, add hot cream, and whisk or blend with an immersion blender until mixture is smooth. Add liqueur, if using, and continue whisking or blending until incorporated. Pour chocolate fondue into a serving bowl and keep warm until ready to serve.

For the garnish, just before serving, combine whipping cream with mascarpone in a small saucepan. Heat gently, whisking constantly, until combined and warm.

Skewer cake pieces and strawberry wedges on wooden skewers, and top with a dollop of cream, a sprig of mint, and some toasted almonds. Serve with chocolate fondue for dipping. You may use other fresh fruit, such as sliced banana, pineapple chunks, orange segments, or sliced pears, instead of or in addition to the strawberries.

Raspberry Dark Hot Chocolate

1½ cups (375 mL) fresh or frozen raspberries

3.6 oz (100 g) 70% dark chocolate, finely chopped

1 cup (250 mL) whipping cream

GARNISH

24–36 mini marshmallows

6–12 fresh raspberries

To make raspberry purée, purée fresh raspberries or thawed frozen raspberries in a food processor, then strain out the seeds using a fine-mesh sieve. You'll need 1 cup (250 mL) of raspberry purée.

Place chocolate in a tall, narrow container. Bring raspberry purée and whipping cream to a boil in a saucepan. Remove from the heat and pour over chocolate. Blend with an immersion blender until well combined and frothy. Place a few pieces of marshmallow in each of 6 serving glasses and lightly caramelize using a blowtorch. Top with 1 or 2 fresh raspberries per glass. Pour hot chocolate on top and serve at once.

Choco-Malt Milkshake with Caramel Bananas

CARAMEL BANANAS

3 Tbsp (45 g) granulated sugar

3 Tbsp (45 mL) water

3 Tbsp (45 g) salted butter

1 Tbsp (15 mL) whipping cream

2 bananas, cubed

pinch of cinnamon

MILKSHAKE

1 cup (250 mL) whipping cream

1 cup (250 mL) 2% milk

8.8 oz (250 g) 70% dark chocolate, finely chopped

½ cup (70 g) malt powder

3 Tbsp + 2 tsp (20 g) instant coffee powder

½ cup (125 g) vanilla ice cream

For the bananas, combine sugar and water in a large saucepan. Bring to a boil over medium heat, then cook without stirring until mixture is caramel in color, 5 to 10 minutes. Remove saucepan from heat. Stir in butter and whipping cream, then add bananas and cinnamon. Cook, tossing gently, until bananas are evenly coated with sauce.

For the milkshake, in a saucepan, bring whipping cream and milk to a boil. In a bowl, combine chocolate, malt powder, and instant coffee. Pour hot cream mixture on top and, using an immersion blender, blend until combined. Let cool in the fridge.

Just before serving, blend chocolate mixture with vanilla ice cream until smooth. Serve at once alongside the Caramel Bananas.

Frozen Chocolate Soufflé

½ cup (125 mL) 2% milk

½ cup (100 g) granulated sugar

3 large egg yolks

5.4 oz (150 g) 70% dark chocolate, finely chopped

2 large egg whites

1 Tbsp + 1 tsp (20 g) granulated sugar

½ cup (125 mL) whipping cream, whipped to soft peaks

GARNISH

Chocolate Egg Nest made with dark chocolate (see page 115)

2 Tbsp (30 mL) Dark Chocolate Sauce (see page 109)

Chocolate Velour (see page 119)

Prepare 6 ramekins by making sleeves out of plastic acetate (see page 116) to go around the outside of the ramekins. The sleeves should extend 1 inch (2.5 cm) above the rim of the ramekins. Wrap around ramekins and secure them with tape or an elastic band.

In a saucepan, bring milk and half the first amount of sugar to a boil over high heat. Combine egg yolks and remaining sugar in a bowl and whisk until mixture is cream colored. Slowly add hot milk mixture to egg yolk mixture, whisking constantly until well combined, and transfer into a heatproof bowl. Place bowl over a saucepan of hot (not boiling) water and cook, whisking often, until mixture is thick enough to coat the back of a spoon, about 10 minutes. Let cool briefly. Whisk constantly and vigorously with a wire whip while adding chocolate, 2 to 3 Tbsp (30 to 45 mL) at a time, until all chocolate is added and mixture is smooth, light in texture, and cooled.

Using an electric mixer, beat egg whites on low speed until they hold soft peaks. Turn mixer to highest speed and add second amount of sugar, continuing to beat until firm, glossy peaks form. Fold one-third of whipped cream into chocolate mixture using a rubber spatula. Gently fold in egg white meringue and remaining whipped cream. Pipe or spoon mixture into prepared ramekins and freeze overnight. Peel off acetate sleeves and decorate using suggested garnishes.

Mini Chocolate Soufflé Cakes

⅓ cup (80 mL) 2% milk

2 Tbsp (15 g) cocoa powder

1 Tbsp (10 g) all-purpose flour

1½ tsp (8 mL) Gelatin Mix (see page 109)

0.6 oz (15 g) 70% dark chocolate, finely chopped

3 large egg yolks

¼ cup + 1 Tbsp (65 g) granulated sugar

1½ large egg whites

¼ cup (50 g) turbinado sugar

Use 1½-inch (3.75 cm) round, flexible silicone molds or nonstick minimuffin tins.

In a saucepan over medium heat, warm milk, cocoa, and flour and cook, stirring constantly, until mixture thickens to the consistency of stirred custard. Remove from the heat. Stir in Gelatin Mix and chocolate.

In a bowl, whisk egg yolks with about half the granulated sugar (2 or 3 Tbsp/about 30 g). Place bowl over a saucepan of simmering (not boiling) water on medium heat and whisk until mixture becomes a thick foam. Fold into chocolate mixture.

Using an electric mixer, beat egg whites until they form soft peaks. Turn the mixer to the highest speed and add remaining sugar, continuing to beat until firm, glossy peaks form. Using a rubber spatula, fold one-third of egg white mixture into chocolate mixture to loosen. Fold in remaining egg white mixture until ingredients are well combined.

Pour batter into silicone molds or muffin tins to a depth of ½ inch (1 cm). Smooth tops as flat as possible. Freeze for at least 4 hours (overnight is best).

To bake, preheat the oven to 350°F (180°C). Remove frozen cakes from molds and place on a tray lined with parchment paper or a silicone mat. Sprinkle each with turbinado sugar and bake for 10 to 15 minutes. Serve immediately.

Coconut & Lime White Hot Chocolate

3.6 oz (100 g) white chocolate, finely chopped

⅔ cup (160 mL) unsweetened coconut milk

⅔ cup (160 mL) whipping cream

¼ cup (60 mL) lime juice

GARNISH

fresh mango, sliced

rasped lime zest

fresh ginger, rasped

coconut, toasted

Place white chocolate in a tall, narrow container. In a saucepan, bring coconut milk and whipping cream to a boil. Add lime juice. Pour hot mixture over chocolate and blend with an immersion blender until well combined and frothy. Pour into warm cups or glasses to serve.

Toss mango slices with lime zest, ginger, and toasted coconut. Serve at once with hot chocolate (as shown).

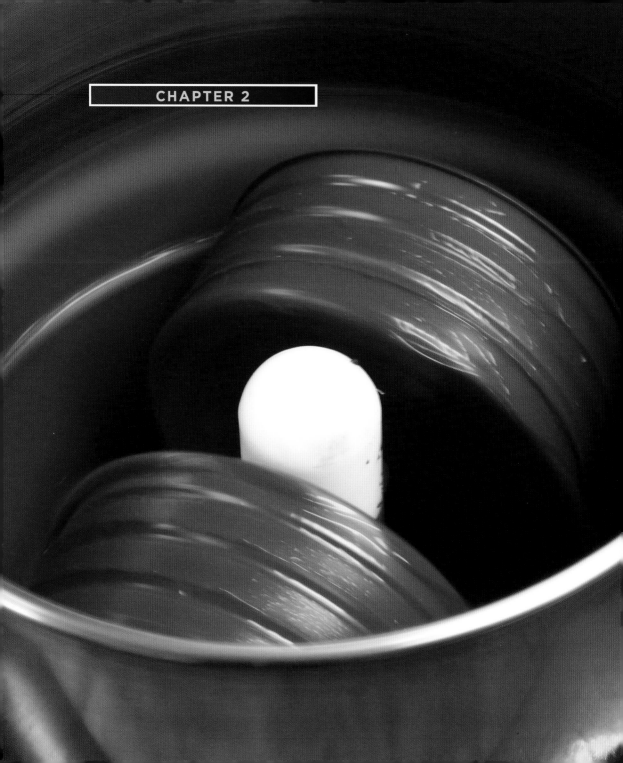

Mousses & Creams

Milk Chocolate & Ginger Panna Cotta

1 cup (250 mL) whipping cream

1 cup (250 mL) orange juice

1 tsp (5 mL) finely grated fresh ginger

3 Tbsp (45 g) Gelatin Mix (see page 109)

4.4 oz (125 g) milk chocolate, finely chopped

GARNISH

Chocolate Angel Hair made with dark
chocolate (see page 115)

1 or 2 oranges, peeled and segmented

candied ginger, cubed

In a saucepan, bring whipping cream, orange juice, and ginger almost to a boil. Remove from the heat, add Gelatin Mix, and stir with a rubber spatula until completely dissolved. Add chocolate and continue mixing until combined. Strain mixture into a measuring cup and divide evenly among serving cups or glasses. Place panna cotta in the fridge for at least 4 hours, or until set (overnight is best). To serve, decorate with garnishes as shown.

Dark Chocolate Pots de Crème

2 cups (500 mL) whipping cream

6 egg yolks

2 Tbsp (30 g) granulated sugar

2 tsp (10 mL) rasped lime zest

pinch of salt

3.6 oz (100 g) 70% dark chocolate, melted

GARNISH

6 fresh raspberries

6 sprigs mint

Warm whipping cream in a saucepan over low heat. In a bowl, combine egg yolks, sugar, lime zest, and salt and whisk until well mixed. Slowly pour (temper) warm cream over yolk mixture, whisk until combined, and transfer mixture into a heat-proof bowl. Place bowl over a saucepan of hot (not boiling) water and cook, whisking constantly, until mixture is thick enough to coat the back of a spoon, and no longer liquidy or foamy, about 10 minutes. Remove from the heat and strain mixture. Add melted chocolate and stir until mixture is smooth.

Divide mixture evenly into 6 serving cups or small ramekins. Place the pots de crème in the fridge for at least 3 hours, or until set (overnight is best). Top with garnishes.

Anise Millefeuille with Dark Chocolate Mousse

½ lb (225 g) puff pastry dough (store-bought)

¼ cup (50 g) granulated sugar

1 tsp (5 mL) anise seeds, crushed

DARK CHOCOLATE MOUSSE

1 recipe (1 cup/250 mL) Custard Cream, warmed (see page 110)

5.4 oz (150 g) 70% dark chocolate, melted

1½ cups (375 mL) whipped cream

Cut dough in half and roll each half into a 10-inch (25 cm) square. Place dough on a baking sheet lined with parchment paper or a silicone mat and prick it all over with a fork. Lightly brush top of dough with some water, sprinkle with sugar and anise seeds, and bake according to package instructions. Let cool on a wire rack.

Whisk warm Custard Cream with melted chocolate until combined. Let cool for a few minutes. Add one-third of whipped cream and whisk until combined. Gently fold in remaining whipped cream using a rubber spatula.

Cut each puff pastry square into 3- × 1½-inch (7.5 × 3.75 cm) strips. Pipe or spoon mousse onto 1 strip, top with another strip, and top that strip with more mousse. Finish with a plain strip of pastry for the top. Serve at once for best texture or store in the fridge for a maximum of 2 hours before serving.

White Chocolate & Macadamia Mousse

¾ cup (175 g) plain yogurt

2 Tbsp (30 g) Gelatin Mix (see page 109)

6.3 oz (180 g) white chocolate, melted

1 Tbsp (15 mL) dark rum (optional)

4 Tbsp (40 g) macadamia nuts, toasted and coarsely chopped

12 banana chips, finely crushed (store-bought)

1 cup (250 mL) whipped cream

GARNISH

Chocolate Teardrops made with dark chocolate (see page 118)

pineapple and mango, cubed

6–12 banana chips

6 sprigs mint

Heat one-third of yogurt in a microwave oven on high in 20-second intervals until hot. Add Gelatin Mix and stir until completely dissolved. Add melted chocolate, remaining yogurt, rum, macadamia nuts, and banana chips and whisk until thoroughly combined. Let mixture cool for a few minutes. With a rubber spatula, fold in whipped cream. Divide mixture among 6 serving glasses or dishes and place in fridge for at least 3 hours, or until set (overnight is best). Serve with garnishes as shown.

Milk Chocolate, Lemon & Peanut Cream

4 large egg yolks

¼ cup (50 g) granulated sugar

2 tsp (10 mL) rasped lemon zest

2 cups (500 mL) whipping cream

½ cup (125 g) smooth peanut butter

5.4 oz (150 g) milk chocolate, melted

GARNISH

Chocolate Angel Hair made with dark chocolate (see page 115)

3.6 oz (100 g) peanuts, roasted

Whisk together egg yolks, sugar, and lemon zest in a medium heatproof bowl until well combined. Meanwhile, bring whipping cream to a boil in a small saucepan over medium-high heat. Slowly add hot cream to egg yolk mixture, whisking constantly until well combined. Whisk in peanut butter until incorporated. Place bowl over a saucepan of hot (not boiling) water and cook, whisking often, until mixture is thick enough to coat the back of a spoon, and no longer liquidy or foamy, about 10 minutes. Remove bowl from heat. Strain mixture into a measuring cup, add melted chocolate, and stir until mixture is smooth.

Divide mixture evenly among 6 serving dishes or glasses. Cover each dish loosely with plastic wrap, then refrigerate for at least 4 hours (overnight is best). Arrange garnishes on top as shown.

Chocolate Chiboust Cream with Nectarine Salad

1 recipe (1 cup/250 mL) Custard Cream
(see page 110)

6 large egg whites

6 Tbsp (90 g) granulated sugar

8.8 oz (250 g) 70% dark chocolate, melted

GARNISH

1 or 2 nectarines, pitted and sliced

maple syrup and peach liqueur (optional)

Chocolate Sugar Bark made with white
chocolate (see page 117)

6 sprigs mint

Make Custard Cream following the recipe on page 110 and keep warm, covered with a sheet of plastic wrap.

Using an electric mixer, beat egg whites on low speed until they hold soft peaks. Turn mixer to highest speed and add sugar, continuing to beat until meringue forms firm and glossy peaks. Fold one-third of meringue into hot Custard Cream. Add melted chocolate and stir until combined. Fold in remaining meringue quickly to avoid forming unmixed clumps of egg whites.

For best results, cream should be used immediately, poured or piped into serving dishes or glasses. Optionally, pipe mixture into flexible molds (2 inches/5 cm in diameter) and freeze for 3 to 4 hours. A couple of hours before serving, unmold chiboust cream onto plates and keep in the fridge until ready to serve.

Toss nectarine slices with some maple syrup and peach liqueur, if desired, and serve with chiboust cream, garnishing with Chocolate Sugar Bark and mint springs.

CHAPTER 3

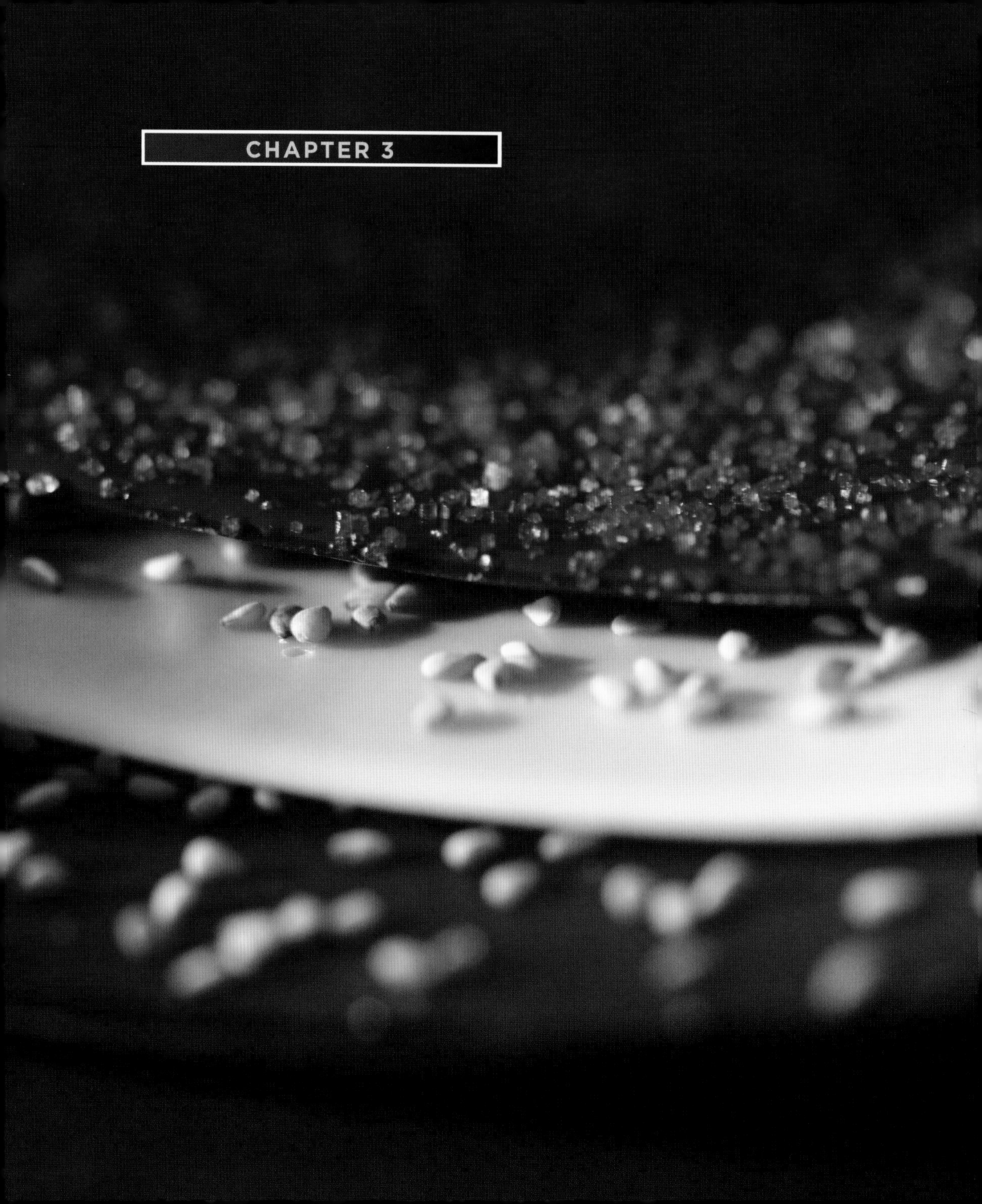

Wedges & Slices

Brownies with Peanut Butter Cream

BROWNIES

8.8 oz (250 g) 70% dark chocolate, chopped

¾ cup + 1 Tbsp (200 g) salted butter

3 large eggs

1½ cups (300 g) granulated sugar

1 tsp (5 mL) vanilla extract

⅔ cup + 3 Tbsp (130 g) all-purpose flour, sifted

2 Tbsp + 1 tsp (20 g) cocoa powder, sifted

1 cup (130 g) peanuts, roasted and crushed

PEANUT BUTTER CREAM

0.9 oz (25 g) 70% dark chocolate, finely chopped

4 tsp (25 g) smooth peanut butter

1 cup (250 mL) whipping cream

GARNISH

Chocolate Plaquettes (milk chocolate, page 116)

Chocolate Curls (page 119)

Caramelized Nuts made with peanuts (page 110)

Preheat the oven to 350°F (180°C).

For the brownies, melt chocolate and butter in a bowl over a saucepan of hot (not boiling) water, stirring occasionally. Take it off the heat. In a separate bowl, whisk eggs and sugar until mixture is homogenous and thick. Add vanilla, and mix. Add egg mixture to chocolate mixture and whisk until smooth. Slowly add flour and cocoa powder, folding them in with a rubber spatula, but do not overmix. Briefly fold in peanuts.

Transfer mixture into a 10-inch (25 cm) square pan lined with parchment paper and bake for about 35 minutes. Let cool before cutting into desired shapes.

For the peanut butter cream, place chocolate and peanut butter in a tall, narrow container. In a saucepan, bring whipping cream to a boil. Remove from the heat and pour over chocolate and peanut butter. Blend with an immersion blender until well combined. Let cool in the fridge. Once cool, using electric mixer, whip the mixture until it forms medium peaks. Serve brownies topped with peanut butter cream and garnishes as shown.

Chocolate Pecan Tart

3 large eggs

½ cup (170 g) corn syrup

¾ cup (150 g) granulated sugar

5 Tbsp (75 g) salted butter, melted

½ recipe Chocolate Tart Dough (see page 109)

1½ cups (180 g) pecan pieces

GARNISH

*½ cup (125 mL) Dark Chocolate Sauce
(see page 109)*

*Chocolate Curls made with dark chocolate
(see page 119)*

whipped cream, sweetened to taste

Preheat the oven to 350°F (180°C).

In a large bowl, whisk together eggs, corn syrup, and sugar. Add melted butter and continue whisking until all ingredients are incorporated and mixture is smooth. Set aside. Roll Chocolate Tart Dough to a thickness of about ¼ inch (6 mm) and press into a 9-inch (22.5 cm) tart pan (or in individual tart pans, if desired). Top with pecan pieces and cover with filling.

Place pan on a baking sheet and bake for approximately 45 minutes. Turn tray around and bake for another 15 to 20 minutes. Let tart cool completely on a wire rack before unmolding. To serve, adorn with garnishes as shown.

Baked Chocolate Custard Pudding

¾ cup + 1 Tbsp (200 g) salted butter

4.6 oz (130 g) 70% dark chocolate, chopped

1 medium-sized (3.6 oz/100 g) banana, peeled and puréed

3 large eggs

¼ cup + 2 Tbsp (80 g) granulated sugar

GARNISH

1 recipe Caramel Bananas (see page 18)

ChocoNut Bark made with milk chocolate and sesame seeds (see page 117)

Preheat the oven to 300°F (150°C). Line a 9-inch (22.5 cm) square baking pan with silicone paper.

In a microwavable container, melt butter and chocolate together. In a bowl, combine puréed banana with eggs and sugar. Add banana mixture to chocolate mixture and stir until thoroughly combined. Pour mixture into prepared pan and place pan in a water bath. Bake for 25 to 30 minutes, or until set. Let cool, then set in the fridge for at least 1 hour before unmolding from pan. Cut into desired shapes and serve either cold or warm with Caramel Bananas and ChocoNut Bark.

Flourless Chocolate Cake with Chantilly

8 large eggs, separated, at room temperature

2 Tbsp (30 g) granulated sugar (for egg yolks)

¼ cup + 1 Tbsp (65 g) granulated sugar (for egg whites)

8.8 oz (250 g) 70% dark chocolate, melted

½ cup (125 g) unsalted butter, melted

GARNISH

1 recipe Chocolate Chantilly (see page 70)

Chocolate Curls made with white chocolate (see page 119)

6–8 fresh strawberries, hulled and cubed

6–8 sprigs mint

Preheat the oven to 325°F (160°C). Line a 12- × 16-inch (30 × 40 cm) baking sheet with parchment paper or a silicone mat.

Separate egg yolks and whites into 2 bowls. Using an electric mixer, whip yolks with first amount of sugar until light and fluffy, and set aside. Using an electric mixer, beat egg whites on low speed until they hold soft peaks. Turn mixer to highest speed and add second amount of sugar, continuing to beat until firm and glossy peaks form. Whisk melted chocolate and butter into egg yolk mixture. Add one-third of egg white mixture and whisk. Fold in remaining egg white mixture with a rubber spatula.

Spread mixture evenly on prepared baking sheet and bake for 10 to 12 minutes. Let cool on a wire rack. Place in the fridge for about 2 hours to chill before cutting into desired shapes.

Pipe or spoon some Chocolate Chantilly on top of cake and garnish with Chocolate Curls, strawberries, and mint.

Raspberry Tarte au Chocolat

10.6 oz (300 g) 70% dark chocolate, finely chopped

1 cup (250 mL) whipping cream

½ cup (125 mL) milk

2 large eggs

½ recipe Chocolate Tart Dough (see page 109)

3 Tbsp (45 mL) raspberry jam

GARNISH

Chocolate Teardrops made with white chocolate (see page 118)

3–4 dozen fresh raspberries

6–8 sprigs mint

Preheat the oven to 350°F (180°C).

Place chocolate in a bowl. Bring cream and milk to a boil in a saucepan and pour over chocolate. Using a wooden spoon or rubber spatula, stir mixture from the center out in a circular motion until chocolate is melted and ingredients are well combined. In a cup, quickly beat eggs with a fork. Add to chocolate mixture and continue mixing until incorporated.

Roll Chocolate Tart Dough to a thickness of about ¼ inch (6 mm) and place dough in a 9-inch (22.5 cm) tart pan (or in individual tart pans, if desired). Cover dough with a sheet of parchment paper, fill cavity with dried beans or rice, and blind-bake the tart for 15 to 20 minutes. Remove from the oven and remove the paper and beans or rice.

Using an offset spatula or a spoon, spread raspberry jam evenly on the top of the tart. Cover with chocolate mixture and bake for about 30 minutes, or until cream is set. Let tart cool completely on a wire rack before unmolding. Garnish with white Chocolate Teardrops, raspberries, and mint.

Hazelnut Chocolate Mousse Pâté

6 large egg yolks

½ cup (100 g) granulated sugar

9 large egg whites

¼ cup + 2 tsp (60 g) granulated sugar

½ cup (50 g) finely ground hazelnuts

¼ cup (40 g) all-purpose flour, sifted

¼ cup + 2 tsp (40 g) cocoa powder, sifted

½ cup (125 g) unsalted butter, melted

1 recipe Dark Chocolate Mousse (see page 32)

1 cup (250 mL) Dark Chocolate Sauce, warmed (see page 109)

GARNISH

Chocolate Sugar Bark made with milk chocolate (see page 117)

Preheat the oven to 350°F (180°C). Line a 13- × 18-inch (33 × 45 cm) baking sheet with parchment paper or a silicone mat.

Using an electric mixer, whip egg yolks with first amount of sugar until light and fluffy. Set aside. Using an electric mixer, beat egg whites on low speed until they hold soft peaks. Turn mixer to highest speed and add second amount of sugar, continuing to beat until firm and glossy peaks form. Using a spatula, fold ground hazelnuts, flour, and cocoa powder into egg yolk mixture. Mix one-quarter of beaten egg white mixture with melted butter and fold into cake mixture. Fold in remaining egg white mixture until just incorporated (do not overmix).

Spread mixture on prepared baking sheet and bake for 20 to 25 minutes. Let cool before removing parchment or mat.

Line a pâté or terrine mold with plastic wrap. Cut strips of cake the same size as the bottom of the mold and build the pâté by alternating layers of cake and Dark Chocolate Mousse until mold is completely filled (make sure to end with cake as the last layer). For best results, place mold in the freezer for about 2 hours, or until firm. Peel plastic off, coat pâté with Dark Chocolate Sauce, and let set in the fridge for at least 1 hour before serving. Garnish with Chocolate Sugar Bark.

Moist Chocolate Minicakes

1 cup (200 g) granulated sugar

1 cup (150 g) all-purpose flour

⅓ cup + 1 Tbsp (50 g) cocoa powder

1 tsp (5 mL) baking soda

½ tsp (2.5 mL) baking powder

¼ tsp (1.25 mL) salt

1 large egg

½ cup (125 mL) buttermilk

½ cup (125 mL) strong brewed coffee

¼ cup (60 mL) peanut oil

½ tsp (2.5 mL) vanilla extract

GARNISH

Chocolate Sugar Sticks made with white chocolate (see page 118)

1 recipe Chocolate Chantilly (see page 70)

fresh small herbs of your choice (optional)

Preheat the oven to 350°F (180°C). Use 3-inch (7.5 cm) round flexible silicone molds, or nonstick or greased muffin tins.

In a bowl, sift dry ingredients together. Mix briefly with a whisk and make a well in the center. In another bowl, combine all wet ingredients, mix briefly with a whisk, and pour into dry ingredients. Whisk all ingredients together until mixture is smooth and homogenous, but do not overmix.

Pour batter into silicone molds or muffin tins. Bake for 25 to 30 minutes. Flip molds or tins onto a wire rack and let cool. Garnish with sugar sticks, chantilly, and herbs.

CHAPTER 4

Bites & Treats

Chocolate Florentines with Honey, Nuts & Fruit

YIELDS 50

½ cup (125 mL) whipping cream

¾ cup (150 g) granulated sugar

⅓ cup (100 g) honey

3 Tbsp (45 g) salted butter

¾ cup (120 g) dried apricots

¼ cup (40 g) dried blueberries

⅓ cup (50 g) sweetened dried cranberries

1½ cups (200 g) sliced almonds

3 Tbsp (30 g) all-purpose flour

tempered dark chocolate for enrobing
or dipping (see page 8)

Preheat the oven to 350°F (180°C).

In a large saucepan, combine whipping cream, sugar, honey, and butter and bring to a boil. Cook to 250°F (120°C), using a candy thermometer to measure temperature, stirring occasionally.

Chop apricots into small cubes and place in a large stainless steel bowl. Add remaining dried fruits, almonds, and flour, and toss together until well mixed. Pour hot whipping cream mixture on top of fruits and nuts and stir until well combined.

Using 2-inch (5 cm) round, flexible silicone molds or nonstick minimuffin tins, place 2 tsp (10 mL) of mixture in each mold or muffin cup, and bake for about 15 minutes. Let cool before removing from molds and placing on tray lined with parchment paper or a silicone mat.

Dip the bottom of each florentine in tempered dark chocolate by holding the top with your fingers. Transfer onto a sheet of parchment paper or food-grade plastic. Once chocolate is set, serve the same day, or store for up to 2 weeks in an airtight container.

Citrus Milk Chocolate Crunch

5.4 oz (150 g) milk chocolate, melted

2 Tbsp (30 g) unsalted butter, melted

¼ cup (50 g) nut butter (almond, pecan, pistachio, or walnut)

2 Tbsp (30 g) candied citrus peel, chopped (store-bought)

¼ tsp (1.25 mL) cinnamon

2 cups (60 g) puffed rice

6.3 oz (180 g) milk chocolate, melted

3 Tbsp (45 g) unsalted butter, melted

GARNISH (OPTIONAL)

candied citrus peel

Line a 10-inch (25 cm) square pan with plastic wrap. Stir first amounts of melted chocolate and butter together. Add nut butter, candied peel, and cinnamon, and mix until combined. Fold in puffed rice and stir until rice is coated with chocolate mixture. Press mixture evenly into prepared pan and allow to set about 1 hour.

Combine second amounts of melted chocolate and butter in a bowl and stir, using a rubber spatula, until well combined. Pour on top of puffed rice mixture and spread evenly with a spatula. Let set until chocolate is firm to the touch. Cut with a serrated knife into 1½-inch (3.75 cm) squares. Serve as is or garnish with candied citrus peel. Store for up to 2 weeks in an airtight container.

Dark Chocolate Banana Jam

4 medium-sized bananas, peeled and mashed

1 cup (200 g) granulated sugar

2 Tbsp (30 mL) orange juice

½ tsp (2.5 mL) ground cardamom, toasted

3.6 oz (100 g) 70% dark chocolate,
finely chopped

Combine bananas, sugar, orange juice, and cardamom in a large saucepan and cook on medium heat for about 5 minutes (or, if you have a sugar refractometer, until it measures 57%). Place chocolate in a tall, narrow container. Pour banana mixture over chocolate and blend with an immersion blender until mixture is smooth. Pour mixture into a clean container fitted with a lid and store in fridge for up to 3 weeks.

Serve jam with sliced brioche, challah, or other sweet bread.

Milk Chocolate Caramel Spread

½ cup (125 mL) water

1¾ cups (350 g) granulated sugar

1¼ cups (310 mL) whipping cream

2 Tbsp (30 g) salted butter

7.2 oz (200 g) milk chocolate, finely chopped

Combine water and sugar in a saucepan and cook on high heat (without stirring) until a candy thermometer reads 340°F (170°C), or mixture turns a golden caramel color. This can take anywhere from 5 to 10 minutes depending on your stove and the type of saucepan you are using. Remove saucepan from heat and, standing back in case mixture splatters, stir in whipping cream and butter with a long-handled spoon. Return saucepan to medium heat and cook, stirring, until all sugar is dissolved.

Place chocolate into a tall, narrow container. Pour caramel mixture over chocolate and blend, using an immersion blender, until mixture is smooth. Use warm as a sauce, or pour into a container and store in the fridge for up to 3 weeks.

Serve with banana bread or pound cake, apples, and almonds.

Crispy Chocolate Ravioli

24 Maldon Salt Ganache truffles, but made without salt, and cut but not coated (see page 82)

48 wonton wrappers (4-inch/10 cm square)

6 Tbsp (90 g) butter, melted

2 large egg whites

2 cups (120 g) breadcrumbs, preferably panko

2 cups (500 mL) oil for deep-frying

GARNISH

24 orange slices

24 fresh blackberries

24 sprigs mint

Place the chocolate truffle squares on a tray lined with parchment paper or a silicone mat and freeze for at least 3 hours (overnight is best).

Lay 1 wonton wrapper on a clean, dry surface and brush with melted butter. Place a piece of frozen truffle in the middle of the wonton square. Fold the right side of the wonton over the truffle, then the left. Fold the bottom edge of the wonton over the truffle and roll into a tight parcel. Moisten the top edge of the wonton and press lightly to seal. Place the wrapped truffle on another sheet of wonton and wrap as above, but fold the bottom portion on the opposite side so that you end up with an even thickness of wonton on both sides. Repeat with remaining truffles.

Brush parcels all over with beaten egg white and roll them in breadcrumbs, pressing firmly and making sure all sides are covered. Freeze on baking sheets for 2 hours.

Preheat the oven to 350°F (180°C).

Heat a deep fryer to 350°F (180°C). Drop frozen wonton parcels into hot oil and fry until golden brown. Remove from oil with a slotted spoon and lay on a wire rack over a baking sheet. Place in the oven for a few minutes to finish cooking until centers are hot. Garnish with oranges, blackberries, and mint, and serve warm.

Profiteroles with Chocolate Sauce

YIELDS 36

½ cup (125 mL) water

½ cup (125 mL) 2% milk

½ cup (125 g) unsalted butter

1 tsp (5 g) granulated sugar

pinch of salt

1 cup (150 g) all-purpose flour

5 large eggs

GARNISH

1 recipe Dark Chocolate Mousse (see page 32)

6 Tbsp (90 mL) Dark Chocolate Sauce (see page 109)

macadamia nuts (optional)

Preheat the oven to 375°F (190°C). Line a baking sheet with parchment or a silicone mat.

Combine water, milk, butter, sugar, and salt in a saucepan over medium heat. Once butter is melted, increase heat to high and bring to a boil. Remove pan from heat, add flour, and immediately stir until well combined. Return saucepan to stove over medium heat and continue stirring for about 1 minute to dry the mixture. Remove from heat and beat in eggs one at a time, until mixture is smooth and shiny.

Pipe or spoon mixture onto prepared baking sheet in mounds 1½ inches (3.75 cm) wide. Bake in preheated oven for 15 minutes. Reduce oven temperature to 350°F (180°C) and bake for another 6 to 8 minutes. Remove from the oven and let cool on a wire rack.

When cool, poke a hole in the bottom of each profiterole, pipe some Dark Chocolate Mousse inside, and serve with Dark Chocolate Sauce. Garnish with nuts, if desired.

Leftover profiteroles can be stored frozen for several weeks.

Chocolate Chantilly Meringues

MERINGUES

3 large egg whites

½ cup (100 g) granulated sugar

¾ cup (100 g) icing sugar, sifted

CHOCOLATE CHANTILLY

1.8 oz (50 g) 70% dark chocolate, finely chopped

1 cup (250 mL) whipping cream

GARNISH

Chocolate Angel Hair made with dark chocolate (see page 115)

gold leaf (optional)

Preheat the oven to 275°F (135°C). Line a baking sheet with parchment paper or a silicone mat.

For the meringues, using an electric mixer fitted with a whip attachment, whip egg whites until they form medium peaks. Add granulated sugar and continue whipping until stiff peaks form. Using a rubber spatula, fold icing sugar into egg white mixture. Transfer mixture into a piping bag fitted with a round tip and pipe 1-inch (2.5 cm) rounds onto the prepared baking sheet. Bake for 40 minutes. Reduce the heat to 200°F (100°C) and bake for another hour. Remove from oven and let meringues cool on a wire rack. Store in an airtight container until ready to use.

For the Chocolate Chantilly, place chocolate in a tall, narrow container. Bring whipping cream to a boil in a saucepan. Remove from the heat and pour on top of chocolate. Blend with an immersion blender until well combined. Let cool in the fridge (overnight is best). Once cool, transfer to a bowl, and use an electric mixer fitted with a whip attachment to whip mixture until it forms medium peaks.

Pipe or spoon some Chocolate Chantilly between 2 meringues. Repeat with remaining chantilly and meringues. Garnish with Angel Hair and gold leaf, if desired.

Chocolate "Chips & Salsa"

CHIPS

1 tsp (5 mL) chili powder

1 tsp (5 mL) cocoa powder

3 Tbsp (45 g) butter, melted

0.6 oz (15 g) 70% dark chocolate, melted

6 Asian spring roll wrappers (store-bought)

SALSA

6 strawberries, hulled and cubed

¼ pineapple, peeled, cored, and cubed

1 mango, peeled, pitted, and cubed

12 mint leaves, chopped

honey to taste

Preheat the oven to 350°F (180°C). Line a baking sheet with parchment paper or a silicone mat.

To make chips, in a small bowl, using a spoon, mix chili and cocoa powder with melted butter and chocolate until well combined. Brush mixture onto each spring roll wrapper, on both sides, and cut into desired shapes. Place chocolate wrappers on prepared baking sheet and bake until crispy, about 3 to 5 minutes. Remove from the oven, let cool, and store in an airtight container.

To make salsa, combine all ingredients, toss briefly, and let sit for at least 1 hour in the fridge before serving. Optionally, serve Chocolate Chips & Salsa with some crème fraîche or yogurt on the side.

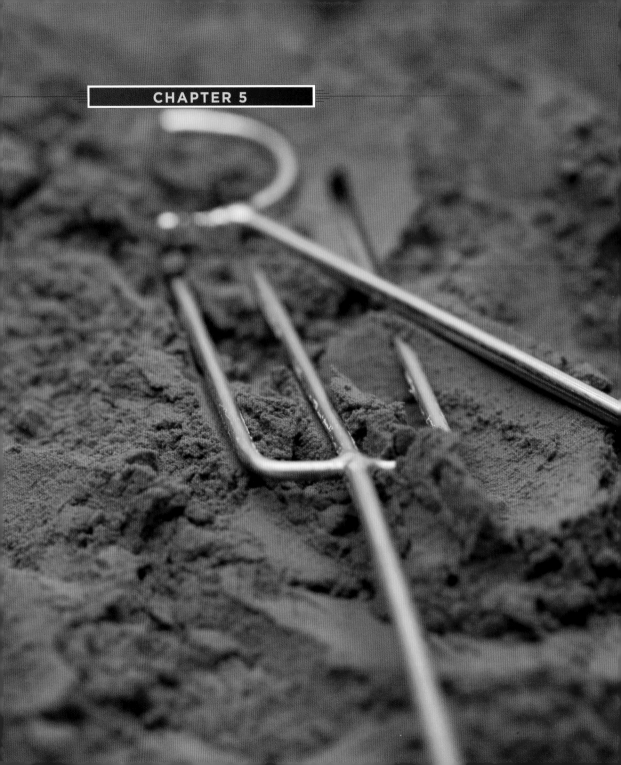

Ganaches & Pralines

Cigarette Cookie Almond Praline

¼ cup (25 g) ground almonds, toasted

¾ cup (195 g) almond butter

½ cup (100 g) berry sugar

4 Tbsp (40 g) cocoa butter, melted

2 dozen (about 4 oz/120 g) cigarette cookies (store-bought), crushed

tempered milk chocolate for enrobing (see page 8)

sliced almonds, toasted, for decorating (optional)

Line an 8-inch (20 cm) square pan with plastic wrap. In a bowl, combine almonds, almond butter, berry sugar, and cocoa butter and mix with a spatula until well combined. Fold in crushed cigarette cookies. Transfer mixture into prepared pan and smooth the top using an offset spatula so that mixture is even. Let set for about 4 hours at room temperature, or until hard (overnight is best).

Unmold praline from pan, peel off plastic wrap, and cut into desired shapes using a knife or cookie cutter. Place the pieces on a tray lined with parchment or a silicone mat to cure for 24 hours at room temperature.

Using a fork, dip pralines into tempered chocolate and slide onto another tray lined with a silicone mat. Optionally, while the chocolate is still wet, finish with 1 or 2 pieces of sliced, toasted almond. Let set for about 4 hours, then store in an airtight container in a cool, dry place for up to 3 weeks.

Fleur de Sel Soft Caramels

1 cup (250 mL) whipping cream

5 Tbsp (75 g) salted butter

1 tsp (5 mL) fleur de sel

1¾ cups + 2 Tbsp (380 g) granulated sugar

¼ cup (60 g) corn syrup

⅓ cup (80 mL) water

1 tsp (5 mL) fresh lemon juice

tempered dark or milk chocolate for enrobing (see page 8)

Line an 8-inch (20 cm) square pan with plastic wrap. Combine whipping cream, butter, and fleur de sel in a saucepan and bring to a boil. Remove from the heat and set aside.

In another saucepan, combine sugar, corn syrup, and water and cook on high heat (without stirring) until a candy thermometer reads 360°F (185°C) or mixture turns a dark caramel color. This can take anywhere from 5 to 10 minutes depending on your stove and the type of saucepan you are using. Remove from the heat and, standing back in case mixture splatters, stir in cream mixture with a long-handled spoon. Return saucepan to high heat and cook, stirring constantly, until candy thermometer reaches 250°F (120°C). Remove from the heat. Add lemon juice and stir until well combined. Pour into prepared pan and let set overnight.

Unmold caramel from pan, peel off plastic wrap, and cut into desired shapes using a lightly oiled knife. Place caramels on a tray lined with parchment paper or a silicone mat. Using a fork, dip caramels into tempered chocolate and slide on another tray lined with a silicone mat. Optionally, while chocolate is still wet, finish with a few grains of fleur de sel. Let set for about 4 hours, then store in an airtight container in a cool, dry place for up to 3 weeks.

Almond, Sesame & Vanilla Praline

1 vanilla bean

1 cup (260 g) almond butter

1 cup (260 g) tahini (sesame butter)

⅓ cup (75 g) granulated sugar

2.8 oz (80 g) 70% dark chocolate, melted

1½ Tbsp (15 g) cocoa butter, melted

1 Tbsp + 1 tsp (20 g) salted butter, softened

¼ cup (30 g) sesame seeds, toasted

tempered dark chocolate for enrobing (see page 8)

sesame seeds, toasted, for decorating (optional)

Line an 8-inch (20 cm) square pan with plastic wrap. Split vanilla bean lengthwise and, with the tip of a knife, scrape out seeds and set them aside. In a bowl, combine almond butter, tahini, sugar, melted chocolate, cocoa butter, and vanilla seeds with a spatula. Add butter and toasted sesame seeds and continue stirring until well mixed. Pour mixture into prepared pan and smooth the top using an offset spatula so that mixture is even. Let set for about 4 hours at room temperature, or until hard (overnight is best).

Unmold praline from pan, peel off plastic wrap, and cut into desired shapes using a knife or cookie cutter. Place pralines on a tray lined with parchment paper or a silicone mat to cure for 24 hours at room temperature.

Using a fork, dip pralines into tempered chocolate and slide onto another tray lined with parchment / silicone. Optionally, while the chocolate is still wet, finish with a few toasted sesame seeds. Let set for about 4 hours, then store in an airtight container in a cool, dry place for up to 3 weeks.

Maldon Salt Ganache

8.5 oz (240 g) 70% dark chocolate, finely chopped

¾ cup + 2 Tbsp (215 mL) whipping cream

2 Tbsp (30 g) corn syrup

1 tsp (5 mL) Maldon salt

¼ cup (60 g) salted butter, softened

tempered dark chocolate for enrobing (see page 8)

½ cup (60 g) roasted cocoa nibs (optional)

Line an 8-inch (20 cm) square pan with plastic wrap. Place chocolate in a bowl. In a saucepan, bring whipping cream, corn syrup, and Maldon salt to a boil and pour mixture over chocolate. For best results, blend using an immersion blender (see Emulsions section on page 11). Or, using a wooden spoon or rubber spatula, stir mixture from the center out in a circular motion, trying not to incorporate any air. When chocolate and cream are thoroughly mixed, add butter and continue blending or stirring until mixture is smooth and shiny. Pour mixture into prepared pan and smooth the top using an offset spatula so that mixture is even. Let set for about 4 hours at room temperature, or until hard (overnight is best).

Unmold ganache from pan, peel off plastic wrap, and cut into desired shapes using a knife or cookie cutter. Place ganache pieces on a tray lined with parchment paper or a silicone mat to cure for 24 hours at room temperature.

Using a fork, dip ganache pieces into tempered dark chocolate and slide onto another tray lined with a silicone mat. Optionally, while chocolate is still wet, finish with a few roasted cocoa nibs. Let set for about 4 hours, then store in an airtight container in a cool, dry place for up to 2 weeks.

Candied Orange Marzipan

2 Tbsp (30 g) candied orange peel, chopped
(store-bought)

17.6 oz (500 g) almond paste

3 Tbsp (45 mL) Grand Marnier

tempered dark chocolate for enrobing
(see page 8)

candied orange peel for decorating

Rinse candied orange peel in cold water for 2 minutes. Drain on a paper towel, and let dry at room temperature on a wire rack for 24 hours.

In a food processor, combine almond paste and Grand Marnier and process for 2 minutes. Add dried orange peel and continue processing for another 45 seconds, or until well combined. Roll the mixture out on parchment paper into a square or rectangular shape, ½ inch (1.25 cm) thick. (For best results, lay a piece of parchment paper on a cutting board. Place mixture on the paper, and to the right and left of the mixture, set 2 pieces of wood, or metal rulers, that are ½ inch/1.25 cm high. Cover with another sheet of parchment paper and, using a rolling pin, roll the mixture, using the rulers as a guide for perfect thickness.) Let rolled-out mixture sit for 6 hours at room temperature, flipping it over halfway through. Cut into desired shapes using a knife or cookie cutter.

Place marzipan pieces on a tray lined with parchment paper or a silicone mat to cure for 24 hours at room temperature. Using a fork, dip marzipan pieces into tempered chocolate and slide onto another tray lined with a silicone mat. While the chocolate is still wet, finish with a few pieces of candied orange peel. Let set for about 4 hours, then store in an airtight container in a cool, dry place for up to 3 weeks.

Passion Fruit, Coconut & Cardamom Ganache

YIELDS 64

11.6 oz (330 g) milk chocolate, finely chopped

pinch of ground cardamom

½ cup (125 mL) passion fruit juice

2 Tbsp (30 g) corn syrup

5 Tbsp (75 g) salted butter, softened

⅓ cup (30 g) unsweetened coconut, toasted and finely ground

tempered milk chocolate for enrobing (see page 8)

cocoa powder for dusting (optional)

Line an 8-inch (20 cm) square pan with plastic wrap. Place chocolate and ground cardamom in a bowl. Bring passion fruit juice and corn syrup to a boil in a saucepan and pour mixture over chocolate. For best results, blend using an immersion blender (see Emulsions section on page 11). Or, using a wooden spoon or rubber spatula, stir the mixture from the center out in a circular motion, trying not to incorporate any air. When chocolate and juice are well mixed, add butter and coconut and continue blending or stirring until mixture is smooth and shiny. Pour mixture into prepared pan and smooth the top using an offset spatula so that mixture is even. Let set for about 4 hours at room temperature, or until hard (overnight is best).

Unmold ganache from pan, peel off plastic wrap, and cut into desired shapes using a knife or cookie cutter. Place ganache pieces on a tray lined with parchment paper to cure for 24 hours at room temperature. Using a fork, dip ganache pieces into tempered chocolate and slide onto another tray lined with a silicone mat. Optionally, while the chocolate is still wet, lightly dust some cocoa powder on a piece of plastic acetate (see page 116) and place on top of truffles.

Let set for about 4 hours, then peel off acetate (if using) and store truffles in an airtight container in a cool, dry place for up to 2 weeks.

Crystallized Ginger Ganache

YIELDS 64

12.5 oz (355 g) milk chocolate, finely chopped

⅔ cup (160 mL) whipping cream

2 Tbsp (30 g) corn syrup

1 Tbsp (15 g) fresh ginger, peeled and finely chopped

¼ cup (60 g) unsalted butter, softened

⅓ cup (50 g) candied ginger, finely chopped

tempered milk chocolate for enrobing (see page 8)

colored sugar, for decorating (optional)

Line an 8-inch (20 cm) square pan with parchment paper or plastic wrap. Place chocolate in a bowl. Bring whipping cream, corn syrup, and fresh ginger to a boil in a saucepan. Let infuse, covered, for about 30 minutes. Strain mixture and bring back to a boil, then pour over chocolate. For best results, blend using an immersion blender (see Emulsions section on page 11). Or, using a wooden spoon or rubber spatula, stir mixture from the center out in a circular motion, trying not to incorporate any air. When chocolate and cream are well mixed, add butter and candied ginger and continue blending or stirring until mixture is smooth and shiny. Pour mixture into prepared pan and smooth the top using an offset spatula so that mixture is even. Let set for about 4 hours at room temperature, or until hard (overnight is best).

Unmold ganache from pan, peel off plastic wrap, and cut into desired shapes using a knife or cookie cutter. Place ganache pieces on a tray lined with parchment paper or a silicone mat to cure for 24 hours at room temperature. Using a fork, dip ganache pieces into tempered chocolate and slide onto another tray lined with a silicone mat. Optionally, while chocolate is still wet, sprinkle with some colored sugar. Let set for about 4 hours, then store in an airtight container in a cool, dry place for up to 2 weeks.

Lemon Macadamia Praline

rasped zest of 1 lemon

1¼ cups (350 g) macadamia nut butter

4.2 oz (120 g) milk chocolate, melted

1 Tbsp (15 g) salted butter, softened

1 cup (130 g) macadamia nuts, toasted and finely chopped

tempered milk chocolate for enrobing (see page 8)

Line an 8-inch (20 cm) square pan with plastic wrap. In a bowl, stir together lemon zest, macadamia nut butter, and melted chocolate with a spatula until well combined. Add butter and continue to stir until incorporated. Pour mixture into prepared pan and smooth the top using an offset spatula so that mixture is even. Completely cover top of mixture with chopped macadamia nuts and tap with back of offset spatula to press nuts in. Let set for about 4 hours at room temperature, or until hard (overnight is best).

Unmold praline from pan, peel off plastic wrap, and cut into desired shapes using a knife or cookie cutter. Place pralines (nut side up) on a tray lined with parchment paper to cure for 24 hours at room temperature. Using a fork, dip pralines into tempered chocolate. Using a blow dryer set on cold air, blow top of chocolate so that nut texture is visible, then slide onto another tray lined with a silicone mat. Let set for about 4 hours, then store in an airtight container in a cool, dry place for up to 3 weeks.

Espresso, Fennel & Sambuca Ganache

7.8 oz (220 g) 70% dark chocolate, finely chopped

1 tsp (5 mL) fennel seeds, toasted and finely ground

¾ cup + 2 Tbsp (215 mL) whipping cream

3 Tbsp (45 g) corn syrup

¼ cup (15 g) ground dark roast coffee beans

3 Tbsp (45 g) salted butter, softened

1 Tbsp (15 mL) sambuca liqueur

tempered dark chocolate for enrobing (see page 8)

Line an 8-inch (20 cm) square pan with plastic wrap. Place chocolate and fennel seeds in a bowl. Bring whipping cream, corn syrup, and ground coffee to a boil in a saucepan. Let infuse, covered, for about 30 minutes. Strain mixture, bring back to a boil, and pour over chocolate. For best results, blend using an immersion blender (see Emulsions section on page 11). Or, using a wooden spoon or rubber spatula, stir the mixture from the center out in a circular motion, trying not to incorporate any air. When chocolate and cream are well combined, add butter and sambuca and continue blending or stirring until mixture is smooth and shiny. Pour mixture into prepared pan and smooth the top using an offset spatula so that mixture is even. Let set for about 4 hours at room temperature, or until hard (overnight is best).

Unmold ganache from pan, peel off plastic wrap or paper, and cut into desired shapes using a knife or cookie cutter. Place ganache pieces on a tray lined with parchment paper to cure for 24 hours at room temperature. Using a fork, dip ganache pieces into tempered chocolate and slide onto another tray lined with a silicone mat. Optionally, while chocolate is still wet, sprinkle with some ground coffee. Let set for about 4 hours, then store in an airtight container in a cool, dry place for up to 2 weeks.

Four-Spice Cocoa Nib Truffles

8.8 oz (250 g) 70% dark chocolate, finely chopped

¼ tsp (1.25 mL) each cinnamon, ancho chili powder, Sichuan pepper, and ground anise seeds

½ cup + 2 Tbsp (150 mL) whipping cream

1 Tbsp (15 g) corn syrup

2 Tbsp (30 g) honey

¼ cup (60 g) salted butter, softened

2 cups (260 g) cocoa nibs, for rolling

tempered dark chocolate for dipping (see page 8)

Place chocolate and spices in a bowl. Bring whipping cream, corn syrup, and honey to a boil in a saucepan and pour mixture over chocolate. For best results, blend using an immersion blender (see Emulsions section on page 11). Or, using a wooden spoon or rubber spatula, stir the mixture from the center out in a circular motion, trying not to incorporate any air. When chocolate and cream are well combined, add butter and continue blending or stirring until mixture is smooth and shiny. Let mixture cool until it becomes the consistency of soft butter. Transfer mixture into a piping bag fitted with a round tube tip, and pipe 64 round-shaped truffles onto a tray lined with parchment paper or a silicone mat. Let truffles cure for 24 hours at room temperature.

Place cocoa nibs in a bowl. Using a fork, dip truffles into tempered chocolate and slide into cocoa nibs. With another fork, sprinkle cocoa nibs over wet chocolate to completely cover. (Dipping and sprinkling is easier with 2 people.) Do not move the chocolate until it sets completely, about 3 to 5 minutes. Shake off excess cocoa nibs and store in an airtight container in a cool, dry place for up to 2 weeks.

CHAPTER 6

New & Modern

Crispy Dark Chocolate Mousse

5.4 oz (150 g) 70% dark chocolate, chopped

5 large egg whites

3 Tbsp (45 g) granulated sugar

3 large egg yolks

food dehydrator

WHITE CHOCOLATE CHANTILLY

3.6 oz (100 g) white chocolate, finely chopped

1 cup (250 mL) whipping cream

GARNISH

Chocolate Egg Nest made with dark chocolate
(see page 114)

6 strawberries, hulled and quartered

fresh, small mint leaves

gold leaf

For the crispy mousse, place chocolate in a bowl over a saucepan of hot (not boiling) water and stir occasionally until completely melted. Using an electric mixer, beat egg whites on low speed until they hold soft peaks. Turn mixer to highest speed and add sugar, continuing to beat until firm and glossy peaks form. Fold egg yolks into egg whites and add melted chocolate, folding quickly to avoid forming unmixed clumps of egg whites.

Using a paper towel, spread a very thin film of oil onto a sheet of plastic acetate (see page 116). Spread a layer of mousse about ½ inch (1.25 cm) thick onto the acetate using an offset spatula, and place the sheet on a food dehydrator tray. Dehydrate the mousse at 145°F (63°C) for 8 to 10 hours, or until crisp. Break or cut into desired shapes and store in an airtight container.

For the chantilly, place white chocolate in a tall, narrow container. Bring whipping cream to a boil in a saucepan. Remove from the heat and pour on top of chocolate. Blend with an immersion blender until well combined. Let cool, then store in the refrigerator for up to 4 days. Once cool, use an electric mixer fitted with a whip attachment to whip the white chocolate mixture until it forms medium peaks. See photo for assembly.

White Chocolate Peanut Pudding

½ cup (125 mL) water

1½ tsp (5 g) agar powder

¼ cup (50 g) granulated sugar

½ cup (125 mL) whipping cream

¼ cup (50 g) honey

1 Tbsp + 2 tsp (25 mL) Gelatin Mix
(see page 109)

5.4 oz (150 g) 36% white chocolate, chopped

1 Tbsp (15 mL) peanut oil

GARNISH

Chocolate Curls made with dark chocolate
(see page 119)

assorted fruits (grapes, blueberries,
blood orange slices, etc.)

6 Tbsp (90 mL) Dark Chocolate Sauce
(see page 109)

roasted peanuts, coarsely chopped

Place water in a tall, narrow container. Mix agar with sugar and add to water, then blend with an immersion blender until well combined. Place agar mixture in a saucepan, add whipping cream and honey, and bring to a boil over medium heat. Blend again with immersion blender until well combined, then continue cooking on medium-high heat for 2 minutes. Remove from the heat. Add Gelatin Mix and stir until dissolved. Transfer mixture into a bowl and refrigerate for about 2 hours, or until set.

Place chocolate and peanut oil in a bowl over a saucepan of hot (not boiling) water. Stir occasionally until completely melted. Cut cream mixture into small pieces and combine with melted chocolate in a high-speed blender. Blend at highest speed until smooth, scraping the sides with a rubber spatula to ensure mixture is completely blended. Strain through a fine-mesh sieve into a bowl. See photo for assembly.

Shaped Dark Chocolate Cream

6.7 oz (190 g) 70% dark chocolate, melted

2 Tbsp (30 mL) water

½ tsp (1.5 g) agar powder

¼ cup + 1 tsp (65 g) corn syrup

2 cups (500 mL) whipping cream

1½ tsp (8 mL) Gelatin Mix (see page 109)

GARNISH

Chocolate Angel Hair made with white chocolate (see page 115)

1 mango, peeled, pitted, and cut into strips

6 strawberries, sliced or cubed

2 fresh oranges, segmented

48 small mint leaves

Line a 9-inch (22.5 cm) square baking pan with plastic wrap. Place chocolate in a large bowl. In a tall, narrow container, blend water and agar using an immersion blender until well combined. In a saucepan, bring agar mixture, corn syrup, and one-third of whipping cream to a boil, whisking constantly. Blend again with immersion blender to make sure all agar is dissolved. Add remaining whipping cream and bring just to a boil. Remove from the heat. Add Gelatin Mix, stir to combine, and pour over chocolate. Blend until chocolate and cream are well combined.

Pour chocolate cream into prepared pan. Refrigerate for at least 1 hour, or until set. Using a ruler and a thin, sharp knife, cut cream into strips and arrange into desired shapes. Serve cold, or warm just before serving in a 225°F (105°C) oven for a few minutes. See photo for assembly.

Semifrozen White Chocolate Foam

½ cup (125 mL) whipping cream

1 medium-sized banana, mashed

2.6 oz (75 g) 36% white chocolate, finely chopped

1 large egg white

1 slab dry ice (about 5 lb/2.2 kg)

siphon dispenser

2 nitrous oxide (N₂O) cartridges

GARNISH

Chocolate Angel Hair made with milk chocolate (see page 115)

rasped zest of 1 lemon

12–18 sweetened dried cranberries, finely chopped

fresh small mint leaves

Bring whipping cream and banana to a boil in a saucepan. Place chocolate in a bowl. Pour cream mixture over chocolate and whisk until well combined. Let cool. Whisk in egg white, then strain entire mixture, discarding solids. Pour liquid into a siphon dispenser. Charge siphon with nitrous oxide cartridges and refrigerate for at least 3 hours (overnight is best).

Just before serving, line the slab of dry ice with parchment paper or a silicone mat. Shake siphon well and dispense some foam onto the dry ice slab. Let foam set for a few seconds, or until bottom part is frozen but top portion is still soft. Remove foam using an offset spatula. Place on a very cold (preferably frozen) plate and serve immediately. See photo for assembly.

Microwave Milk Chocolate Foam Cake

½ cup (50 g) finely ground almonds

3 Tbsp (45 g) granulated sugar

3 Tbsp (30 g) all-purpose flour

5 large egg whites

1.6 oz (45 g) milk chocolate, melted

siphon dispenser

2 nitrous oxide (N₂O) cartridges

GARNISH

Chocolate Curls made with milk chocolate (see page 119)

Dark Chocolate Sauce (see page 109, optional)

Place almonds, sugar, and flour in a food processor and process on high speed. Add egg whites and process until combined. Add melted chocolate and continue to process until mixture is the consistency of whipping cream. Pass mixture through a fine-mesh sieve into a siphon dispenser. Charge siphon with nitrous oxide cartridges, shake well, and refrigerate for 2 hours.

Just before serving, dispense the foam cake mixture into ceramic cups to fill them about halfway, and place in the microwave for about 45 seconds on high heat. Because there are many different types of microwave ovens, we suggest that you make a few extra portions so that you can test cooking time in your microwave and record results for the next time. To unmold foam cakes, run an offset spatula along the wall of the cups. Cut the cake into pieces and serve with suggested garnishes.

CHAPTER 7

Basic Recipes

CHOCOLATE TART DOUGH

Yields 2 tarts, about 9 inches (22.5 cm) each

In a bowl, cream butter and icing sugar with a rubber spatula. Stir in flour and cocoa powder. When almost mixed, add eggs and continue stirring until combined. Wrap dough in a sheet of plastic wrap and refrigerate for at least 2 hours before using.

1 cup + 2 Tbsp (280 g) unsalted butter, softened
2 Tbsp + 1 tsp (35 g) icing sugar
2 cups + 2 Tbsp (320 g) all-purpose flour
¼ cup + 2 tsp (40 g) cocoa powder
2 large eggs

DARK CHOCOLATE SAUCE

Yields 2 cups (500 mL)

In a large bowl, whisk sugar and cocoa powder together until completely mixed. Transfer mixture into a saucepan, add water, and bring to a boil, whisking to prevent scorching. From time to time, skim the foam that forms on the surface using a slotted spoon dipped in cold water. Once mixture has boiled, remove saucepan from heat. Add Gelatin Mix, stir until completely dissolved, and strain mixture into a clean container fitted with a lid. Let cool at room temperature, then refrigerate until needed.

1 cup (200 g) granulated sugar
⅓ cup + 3 Tbsp (65 g) cocoa powder
⅔ cup + 1 Tbsp (175 mL) water
5½ Tbsp (83 g) Gelatin Mix (see below)

GELATIN MIX

Yields ¼ cup (60 mL)

Combine water and gelatin in a microwaveable container. Allow gelatin to bloom for 5 minutes. Microwave on high heat for 20 to 30 seconds, or until melted. Let set at room temperature. Cover container with plastic wrap and store in the fridge for up to 1 week.

¼ cup (60 mL) cold water
1 Tbsp (15 mL) gelatin powder

CUSTARD CREAM

Yields 1¼ cups (375 g)

1 cup (250 mL) 2% milk
¼ cup + 2 tsp (60 g) granulated sugar
3 Tbsp + 2 tsp (25 g) custard powder
or cornstarch
1 large egg

In a heavy saucepan, scald milk with half the sugar. In a bowl, vigorously whisk remaining sugar with custard powder and egg until mixture is smooth and creamy. Pour hot milk into egg mixture a little at a time, whisking constantly. Strain this combined mixture back into the saucepan.

Cook mixture over high heat until it forms bubbles and thickens, stirring constantly with a wire whisk to prevent scorching. Remove from the heat, transfer to a clean container, and cover immediately with plastic wrap, pressed right against the cream. Using the sharp point of a knife, puncture about 6 holes in the plastic to allow steam to escape. Cool and refrigerate. The refrigerated cream will keep for 3 to 4 days.

CARAMELIZED NUTS

Yields about 4.4 oz (125 g)

⅓ cup (75 g) granulated sugar
¼ cup (60 mL) water
3.6 oz (100 g) unsalted nuts, such as
pistachios, almonds, walnuts, or pecans

Preheat the oven to 350°F (180°C).

In a small saucepan over high heat, bring sugar, water, and nuts to a boil. Boil for 2 minutes, then strain through a fine-mesh sieve, discarding liquid. Spread nuts on a baking sheet lined with parchment paper or a silicone mat and bake until golden brown, about 10 to 15 minutes. Let cool completely, then store in an airtight container.

CHOCOLATE FLAVOR MATCHING CHART

Fruits and Berries	DARK	MILK	WHITE
Apricot	X	X	X
Banana	X	X	X
Blackberries			X
Black currants		X	X
Blueberries			X
Boysenberries			X
Cherries	X	X	X
Cranberries			X
Grapes			X
Lemon	X	X	X
Lime			X
Loganberries			X
Mango			X
Orange		X	X
Papaya			X
Passion fruit	X	X	X
Pear	X	X	
Persimmon			X
Pomegranate			X
Raspberries	X	X	X
Sour cherries		X	
Strawberries	X	X	X

Spices and Herbs	DARK	MILK	WHITE
Anise	X	X	
Basil	X	X	X
Cardamom	X	X	X
Chili pepper	X	X	
Cinnamon	X	X	X
Cloves	X	X	
Ginger	X	X	X
Lavender	X	X	
Mint	X	X	X
Nutmeg	X	X	
Salt	X	X	
Vanilla	X	X	X
Verbena	X	X	
Violet	X	X	

	DARK	MILK	WHITE
Nuts, Seeds, and Legumes			
Almonds	X	X	X
Cashews	X	X	X
Cocoa nibs	X	X	X
Coconut	X	X	X
Coffee	X	X	
Hazelnuts	X	X	X
Macadamia nuts		X	X
Peanuts	X	X	X
Pecans	X	X	X
Pistachios	X	X	X
Pumpkin seeds			X
Sesame seeds	X	X	X
Walnuts	X	X	

	DARK	MILK	WHITE
Spirits			
Armagnac	X	X	
Brandy	X	X	
Bourbon	X	X	
Cointreau	X	X	
Kirsch	X	X	
Liqueurs	X		X
Rum, dark or light	X	X	X
Vin Santo	X	X	
Dried Fruits			
Citrus peel	X	X	
Currants	X	X	
Dates	X	X	X
Figs	X	X	X
Prunes			X
Raisins	X	X	

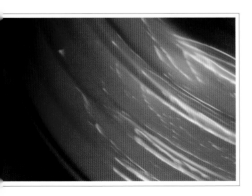

	DARK	MILK	WHITE
Sweeteners			
Butterscotch	X	X	
Caramel	X	X	X
Honey	X	X	
Malt	X	X	
Maple syrup	X	X	
Table and specialty sugars	X	X	X
Dairy			
Cream	X	X	
Cream cheese	X	X	
Crème anglaise	X	X	
Mascarpone	X	X	
Milk	X	X	X
Ricotta	X	X	
Sour cream	X	X	
Unsalted butter	X	X	
Yogurt	X		X

	DARK	MILK	WHITE
Miscellaneous			
Brioche	X	X	
Graham crackers	X	X	
Marshmallows	X	X	
Rice Krispies	X	X	
Tea	X	X	X
Modern			
Bell pepper coulis		X	X
Cheddar cheese	X	X	X
Cilantro	X	X	X
Gruyère		X	X
Olive oil	X	X	X
Pumpkin seed oil	X	X	X
Sherry vinegar	X	X	X
Sweet potato		X	
Tomato	X		X

CHAPTER 8

Decorative Chocolate Techniques & Recipes

CHOCOLATE EGG NEST

Yields about 12 decoration portions

Place a marble tile in the freezer for 1 day. It is important to have everything ready before removing the marble from the freezer, including a piping bag, a tray lined with parchment paper (or a silicone mat), a clean towel or paper towel, and an offset spatula. Fill the piping bag with the chocolate, cut the tip, and quickly pipe thin lines of chocolate up and down the length of the marble until you have a strip about 1 inch (2.5 cm) wide. You need to work quickly, otherwise the chocolate will get too hard and you will not be able to bend it. Slide the offset spatula between the marble and the chocolate. Pick up the chocolate, quickly bend it into the shape of a nest, and place it on the tray lined with parchment paper. Wipe the marble tile with a towel to remove any frost and repeat as many times as needed. It is best to work with 2 people so that you can make more nests before the marble becomes too warm to cool the chocolate. If you have many decorations to make, freeze 2 or more tiles.

8.8 oz (250 g) tempered chocolate (dark, milk, or white)

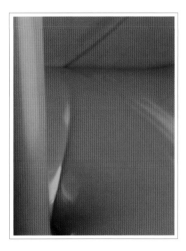

CHOCOLATE ANGEL HAIR

Yields about 12 decoration portions

Place a marble or stainless steel rolling pin in the freezer for 1 day. It is important to have everything ready before removing the rolling pin from the freezer, including a piping bag, a tray

8.8 oz (250 g) tempered chocolate (dark, milk, or white)

See page 8 for instructions on how to temper chocolate.

lined with parchment paper (or a silicone mat), and a clean towel or paper towel. Fill the piping bag with the chocolate, cut a small hole at the tip, and quickly pipe thin lines of chocolate back and forth across the full length of the frozen rolling pin. The faster your piping motion, the thinner the chocolate lines will be. Once the chocolate is hard (30 to 60 seconds), place one end of the rolling pin on the parchment paper–lined tray (or a tray with a silicone mat) and slide 1 hand over the pin to loosen the chocolate onto the tray. Wipe the rolling pin with a towel to remove any frost and repeat as many times as needed. If you have many decorations to make, freeze 2 or more rolling pins.

CHOCOLATE PLAQUETTES

Yields about 24 decoration portions

4.4 oz (125 g) tempered chocolate (dark, milk, or white)

Using an offset spatula, spread tempered chocolate as evenly as possible over a clean sheet of plastic acetate. (Sheets of plastic acetate are available in craft stores, printing shops, and graphic design supply stores.) Cover chocolate with another sheet of acetate and, using an X-Acto knife and ruler, cut the chocolate into desired shapes. To prevent chocolate from warping when hardening, sandwich the chocolate sheet between 2 baking sheets. Let set for at least 1 hour, until fully crystallized, before removing the sheets of plastic acetate from the chocolate.

CHOCOLATE SUGAR BARK

Yields about 24 decoration portions

Using an offset spatula, spread the tempered chocolate as evenly as possible over a clean sheet of plastic acetate (see Chocolate Plaquettes recipe on page 116). While chocolate is still wet, sprinkle it with sugar. Cover chocolate with another sheet of acetate and sandwich the chocolate sheet between 2 baking sheets. Let set for at least 1 hour, until fully crystallized, before removing the sheets of plastic acetate from the chocolate. Break chocolate into desired shapes.

4.4 oz (125 g) tempered chocolate (dark, milk, or white)
¼ cup (50 g) colored sugar, or to taste

CHOCONUT BARK

Yields about 24 decoration portions

Using an offset spatula, spread the tempered chocolate as evenly as possible over a clean sheet of plastic acetate (see Chocolate Plaquettes recipe on page 116). While chocolate is still wet, sprinkle it with nuts or seeds of your choice. Cover chocolate with another sheet of acetate and sandwich the chocolate sheet between 2 baking sheets. Let set for at least 1 hour, until fully crystallized, before removing the sheets of plastic acetate from the chocolate. Break chocolate into desired shapes.

4.4 oz (125 g) tempered chocolate (dark, milk, or white)
¼ cup (30 g) seeds or nuts, toasted and chopped (use more or less to taste)

CHOCOLATE SUGAR STICKS

Yields about 24 decoration portions

4.4 oz (125 g) tempered chocolate (dark, milk, or white)

2 cups (400 g) colored or granulated sugar, or to taste

Fill a piping bag with tempered chocolate and cut a small hole at the tip. On a baking sheet lined with parchment paper, sprinkle enough sugar to evenly cover the tray. Pipe long strands of chocolate the length of the tray. While chocolate is still wet, sprinkle sugar over each strand. Let set for at least 1 hour, until fully crystallized, before removing from baking sheet.

CHOCOLATE TEARDROPS

Yields about 24 decoration portions

4.4 oz (125 g) tempered chocolate (dark, milk, or white)

Fill a piping bag with chocolate and cut a small hole at the tip. Pipe small, round mounds of chocolate (about 1 inch/2.5 cm in diameter) onto a clean sheet of plastic acetate (see Chocolate Plaquettes recipe on page 116). Using the tip of a small painter spatula or dinner knife, drag a line from the center of each mound out to form teardrop shapes. Let set for at least 1 hour, until fully crystallized, before removing chocolates from the sheet of plastic acetate.

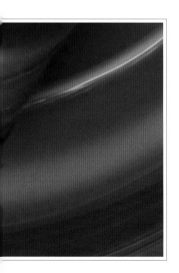

CHOCOLATE CURLS

Yields about 24 decoration portions

Using an offset spatula, spread the tempered chocolate as evenly as possible over a clean sheet of plastic acetate (see Chocolate Plaquettes recipe on page 116). Using a plastic decorating comb (cut ends flat if teeth are pointy), drag the comb over the chocolate so that you end up with strips of chocolate. Roll or twist plastic acetate into a corkscrew shape and secure both ends with a weight or piece of tape. Let set for at least 1 hour, until fully crystallized, before removing the sheets of plastic acetate from the chocolate.

4.4 oz (125 g) tempered chocolate (dark, milk, or white)

CHOCOLATE VELOUR

Yields about 12–24 decoration portions

Combine the chocolate and cocoa butter until completely mixed. Strain mixture into the canister of the spray gun, and spray the chocolate mixture over the item to be decorated as if it were regular paint. To acquire the "velour" effect, the object to be sprayed must be fully frozen.

4.4 oz (125 g) tempered chocolate (dark, milk, or white)
6 Tbsp (60 g) cocoa butter, melted
a clean compressed or airless spray gun

CHAPTER 9

Pairing Wine with Chocolate

There is a lot of controversy about whether wine and chocolate really do go together. Some say that just about any dry red (or white) wine will match with any type of chocolate. And many assume that just about any type of sweet wine, from late harvest to icewine, is a suitable partner for any chocolate, in any form, since these are typically considered dessert wines. Perhaps the main reason for the confusion is the lack of a clear definition of what pairing wine with chocolate means. Does it mean pairing various wines with solid chocolate bars based on the country of origin of the cocoa beans and the percentage of cocoa they contain? Or is the pairing based on whether a dessert is made with dark or milk chocolate? (Note that white chocolate is not really chocolate, as it does not contain any whole cocoa liquor, just cocoa butter.)

In a typical chocolate dessert, like a rich custard-based chocolate mousse, for example, only 40 to 45 percent of its total weight will actually be dark chocolate. A typical chocolate sponge or biscuit will be made with cocoa powder and actually may not contain any whole chocolate liquor at all. Even rich dark chocolate ganache fillings in pralines or bonbons will typically contain only about 40 to 45 percent chocolate by weight.

The traditional wisdom is that wine and chocolate are not suitable partners because the rich sweetness of chocolate is too overpowering for most wines. Such a general statement is misleading, as high-quality dark chocolate bars can be extremely bitter and not sweet at all. Try an 80 to 85 percent bar or even a 90 to 99 percent chocolate bar and, if you are not used to it, you will be begging for sugar! Conversely, milk chocolate typically only contains about 36 percent cocoa liquor and can be very sweet indeed.

As you can see, it's hard to make blanket statements when it comes to pairing chocolate and wine. So our intent is not to offer definitive rules, but rather guidelines to make the process of pairing chocolate and wine easier. As mentioned in our previous books (*Wild Sweets*, pages 41–43 and 55, and *Wild Sweets Chocolate*, pages 176–181), pairing wines can be difficult as not all sweet wines are dessert wines, and not every dessert can be matched with a sweet wine. This is especially important when pairing wine with chocolate desserts. As always, experiment to determine what you like best—and discover for yourself how a well-chosen wine can enhance a well-prepared chocolate dessert. Here is a list of factors to keep in mind:

FLAVOR: As a starting point, we suggest trying to match certain flavors in the wine with similar characteristics in the food. Keep in mind that wine by itself has its own distinct taste and aroma. A wine will taste different when it is combined with food than it will on its own, as elements in the wine interact with those in the food. This metamorphosis can provide very different taste results; some may be great, while others may not be as positive.

FAT: Chocolate is loved for its taste, but also for its melting texture, which varies depending on the amount of cocoa butter in the chocolate bar. If a chocolate bar contains a lot of cocoa butter, it will easily melt at body temperature, which is great when nibbling on a piece of chocolate. However, fat has a cloying effect, so keep in mind that too much cocoa butter fat can be detrimental to wine pairing.

SWEETNESS: To match wine and chocolate, as in matching wine with any dessert, the wine must be sweeter than the dessert. If the dessert is sweeter, the wine will taste thin, uninteresting, and even bitter. Typically, chocolate with concentrated and/or creamy flavors will pair best with sweet, full-bodied, high-alcohol wines, since the alcohol gives the impression of richness and sweetness.

TANNIN: Tannins are a type of polyphenol that have both astringent and bitter tastes. Unprocessed cocoa beans, from which cocoa liquor is extracted to make chocolate, are typically high in tannins. Like wine, the cocoa beans go through a fermentation process that reduces the natural level of tannins. So the higher the percentage of cocoa liquor in the chocolate, the higher the level of tannins it will contain. As a result, it is best to eat a chocolate bar or a rich, dark chocolate dessert by itself, or to serve a wine rich in tannins, but not both together. Paired, they will create an unpleasant, astringent, bitter sensation in the mouth.

The following are a few examples of wine categories to consider as pairing partners to chocolate. There are many more options to consider. The pairing success for these wines (or any other wines, for that matter) will depend, as mentioned above, on the type of chocolate dessert that you are serving. Do keep that in mind when selecting or purchasing wines. Again, experimentation is the key to new discoveries.

FORTIFIED WINES are sweet wines to which a neutral grain spirit is added at a certain point to stop the fermentation process and maintain a high natural sugar content. We find this type of wine the best to pair with chocolate. Here are a few to consider:

SHERRY: Sweet (cream) sherries in particular, with their nutty character, work well with chocolate.

PORT: Tawny port, with its aromas of caramel, coffee, nuts, dried figs, and spices, is probably our favorite wine to pair with chocolate. Tawny ports are well-aged wines, aged for ten, twenty, or even thirty years. And, you guessed it—the older the variety, the better the pairing!

MUSCAT: Sweet fortified wines such as French Muscat Beaumes-de-Venise, California black or orange Muscat, or Australia Liqueur Muscat, with their notes that might include dried fruits, nuts, and spices, also work well with nut- and/or fruit-based chocolate desserts.

LATE HARVEST WINES are made from grapes left on the vine after the usual harvest time. These grapes contain a higher amount of residual sugar and produce sweeter wines. Some of these wines are sometimes infected with a mold called *Botrytis*

cinerea, also known as noble rot. These delicate wines are not well suited to deep, dark chocolate desserts, which will easily overpower them. Although pairing milk chocolate is a challenge due to the chocolate's high dairy content, late harvest wines are a good choice to consider. For example, the botrytis-affected Hungarian Tokaji, with its aromas of butter, honey, apricot, and citrus, can be a great partner for milk chocolate–based desserts, or even less bitter ganaches and creamy truffles. Other choices may include French Sauternes, or German or Austrian Beerenauslese and Trockenbeerenauslese.

SPARKLING WINES are made using several techniques, including the laborious and expensive multistep process called *méthode Champenoise*. A mixture of sugar and spirits, called *dosage*, is added just before the final corking to determine how sweet the sparkling wine or champagne will be. We like to match the texture of light (in texture, but also in fat content) chocolate mousses with the effervescence of sparkling wines. Try an Italian Moscato d'Asti or Asti Spumante, French *doux* (sweet) champagne, or California Crémant.

FRUIT-BASED DESSERT WINES are often made by macerating the fruits (soaking them in alcohol) before fermentation to impart an additional level of flavor concentration. Some of the best fruit wines to pair with chocolate include Framboise (raspberry) and Cassis (black currant), as these fruits are naturally complementary to chocolate in many dessert preparations.

Look for ingredients such as agar and gelatin powder at your local health food store. Results may vary depending on the brand. For the best results, please go to DC DUBY Wild Sweets® Virtual Boutique (www.dcduby.com). We feature many specialty ingredients under the Elements line, including agar powder (ARGUM) and gelatin powder (GELAT), as well as Wild Sweets oRigiNe® high-percentage dark and milk chocolate bars, origin-roasted cocoa nibs, premium commercial-grade origin bulk chocolate, and more. Our exclusive line of artisanal chocolate products and the Elements line are also available wholesale to the retail, gift, and food service sectors.

Our website features cooking videos along with chocolate techniques and tips. We also offer cooking classes and Chocolate Tasting & Appreciation sessions in our Wild Sweets Theatre. For more information, for wholesale inquiries, to purchase products, or to book a seat in one of our classes or tasting sessions, visit the website or call (604) 277-6102.